RKOM

N

2   ged ic
ek a book is overdue

Maths Together

There's a lot more to maths than numbers and sums;
it's an important language which helps us describe, explore and
explain the world we live in. So the earlier children develop
an appreciation and understanding of maths, the better.

We use maths all the time – when we shop or travel from one
place to another, for example. Even when we fill the kettle we are
estimating and judging quantities. Many games and puzzles
involve maths. So too do stories and poems, often
in an imaginative and interesting way.

Maths Together is a collection of high-quality picture books
designed to introduce children, simply and enjoyably, to basic
mathematical ideas – from counting and measuring to pattern and
probability. By listening to the stories and rhymes, talking about
them and asking questions, children will gain the confidence to try
out the mathematical ideas for themselves – an important step
in their numeracy development.

You don't have to be a mathematician to help your child
learn maths. Just as by reading aloud you play a vital role in their
literacy development, so by sharing the *Maths Together* books
with your child, you will play an important part in developing their
understanding of mathematics. To help you, each book has detailed
notes at the back, explaining the mathematical ideas that it
introduces, with suggestions for further related activities.

With *Maths Together*, you can count on doing the
very best for your child.

To Elliot
H. H.

Text first published in Great Britain 1978 by World's Work Ltd, The Windmill Press

This edition published 1999 by Walker Books Ltd, 87 Vauxhall Walk, London SE11 5HJ
by arrangement with Egmont Children's Books Limited, London

2 4 6 8 10 9 7 5 3 1

From 'Abu Ali: Three Tales of the Middle East', text by Dorothy O. Van Woerkom.
Text copyright © 1976 Dorothy O. Van Woerkom
Illustrations © 1999 Harry Horse
Introductory and concluding notes © 1999 Jeannie Billington and Grace Cook

This book has been typeset in ITC Tempus Sans.

Printed in Singapore

British Library Cataloguing in Publication Data
A catalogue record for this book is available from the British Library.

ISBN 0-7445-6833-1 (hb)
ISBN 0-7445-6825-0 (pb)

Abu Ali
Counts His
Donkeys

A Folktale from the Middle East

Retold by
Dorothy O. Van Woerkom

Illustrated by
Harry Horse

WALKER BOOKS
AND SUBSIDIARIES

LONDON • BOSTON • SYDNEY

Abu Ali bought nine donkeys
at the fair.
He climbed on the first donkey.
"Whr-r-r-r!" said Abu Ali.

The donkey began to trot, and the other donkeys followed.

"Now," said Abu Ali, "are all my
donkeys here?"
He turned round and counted.

five ..

four ...

three ...

two ...

"One ...

six ...
    seven ...
        eight ...
            EIGHT donkeys!"

Abu Ali jumped down
from his donkey.

He looked
behind trees,
behind bushes.

No donkey.

"I will count again," he said.

"One …

two …

three …

four …

five …

six …

seven …

eight …

nine …

NINE donkeys!"

Abu Ali climbed back on his donkey.
"Whr-r-r-r! Soon I will be home
with my nine new donkeys."

CLIP, CLAPPETY-CLOP.
CLIP, CLAPPETY-CLOP.

"Now how many donkeys do I have?" Abu Ali counted EIGHT donkeys!

He jumped down
from his donkey.

He looked
behind rocks,
over hilltops.

No donkey.

But when he turned round –
NINE donkeys!

"When I get home," said
Abu Ali, "will I have
nine donkeys, or will
I have eight?"

Abu Ali saw his friend Musa
coming up the road.
"Help me, friend Musa!"
he cried. "I keep losing
a donkey. Now I
have nine.

But when I climb on my donkey – like this –

I have only eight donkeys!"

Musa laughed. "Eight donkeys?
Nine donkeys? Why, I see
TEN donkeys."

"Ten donkeys?" said Abu Ali.
"Where do you see ten donkeys?"

"I see eight donkeys following your donkey.
I see the donkey you are sitting on."
Musa could not stop laughing.

"Oh!" said Abu Ali. "I am sitting on the
ninth donkey! But you said you see ten."

"The tenth donkey is the donkey sitting on YOUR donkey," Musa said.

"Its name is ... Abu Ali!"

About this book

The story of Abu Ali's journey home from the fair helps children to understand two important mathematical ideas: conservation of number and position.

When they are learning to count, it takes children time to realize that the order and position of the objects to be counted make no difference to the total. The pictures in *Abu Ali Counts His Donkeys*, showing the donkeys in a different order every time, help children see this. They will also have the satisfaction of being cleverer than Abu Ali, who keeps forgetting to count one donkey when he's sitting on it.

Each time Abu Ali searches for the missing donkey and checks the total, there are opportunities to use words like *under, behind, above, next to, to the left of,* as well as those of numerical order, e.g. *second, last, third* and *next to the last*. These words are useful when children come to describe *where* something is for themselves.

Later on they will come to describe position in more mathematical ways using angles and distance, sometimes with diagrams and models.

Notes for parents

As you read the story, encourage your child to help Abu Ali count his donkeys. If they are confident with counting you could suggest they start at the blue donkey each time.

Can you start counting with the blue donkey?

I'll try; one...

He looked behind the rocks and over the hills.

I wonder where he'll look next?

Children can use the pictures to retell the story in their own words. This gives them a chance to describe the journey and say where Abu Ali looked for his donkeys.

The donkey with flowers and the blue donkey are very noticeable in the pictures. As you go through the book, you can talk about their order in the line (first, second, last) and their position (behind, in front of, next to).

The one with flowers is second.

He's after Abu Ali, and then there are seven more behind him.

Children follow instructions which involve position all the time – when they're finding things, putting things away, or going somewhere.

Children love treasure hunts. Hide a small object somewhere in the room, and give your child two or three very general clues to where it is. Have the first go yourself to show them how to play, and when it's their turn make sure they don't tell you *exactly* where the object is.

Your child may enjoy making a map of a simple journey to school or to a friend's house. They can draw the map from memory and then add details after they've tried it out.

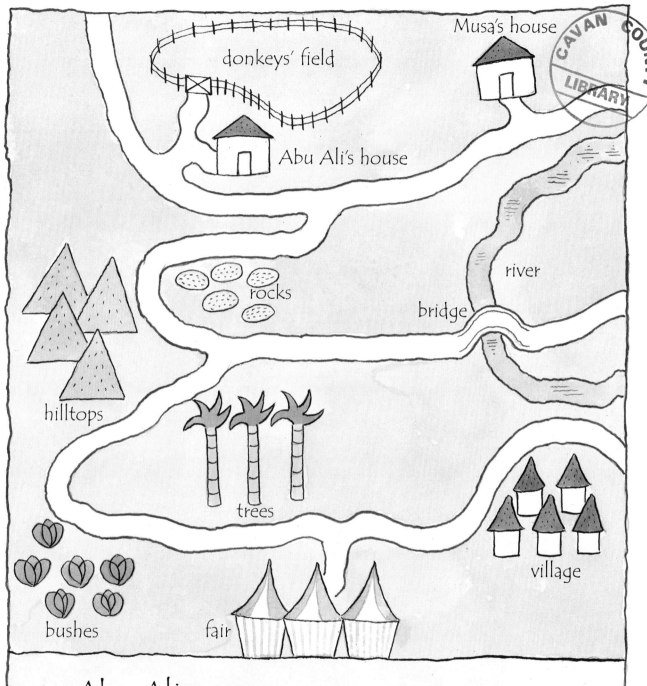

donkeys' field

Musa's house

Abu Ali's house

river

rocks

bridge

hilltops

trees

village

bushes

fair

Abu Ali game

You can use this map to give Abu Ali, Musa and the donkeys directions
home from the fair. Ask your child which way each of them should go
at the junctions. You can use the map to ask other questions too, like
"How can the donkeys go from their field to the bridge?"

Maths Together

The *Maths Together* programme is divided into two sets – yellow (age 3+) and green (age 5+). There are six books in each set, helping children learn maths through story, rhyme, games and puzzles.

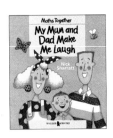

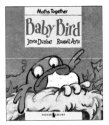